The story of Martha Ann Ricks is quite incredible. She was born as a slave in the United States of America and ended up meeting Queen Victoria and giving her the gift of a quilt that she had made.

Martha was born in Tennessee, in the United States of America, in about 1817. Her mother, father, brother, and sisters were all slaves on a farm.

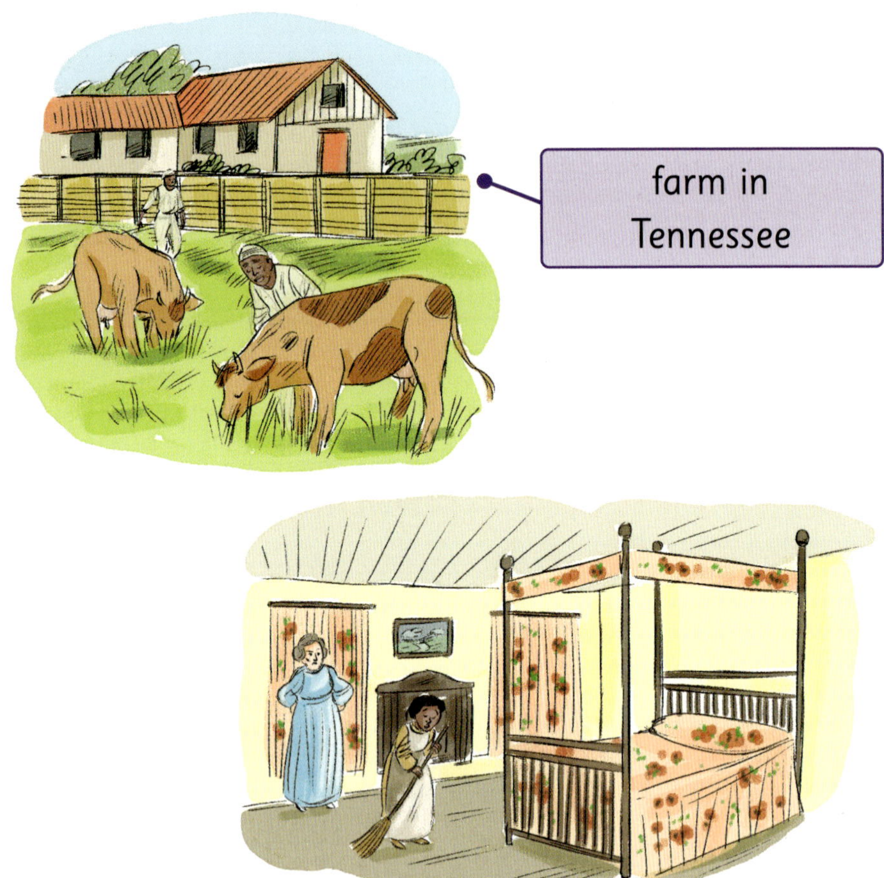

Martha and her brothers and sisters were not allowed to go to school. Her father and brothers were forced to do jobs on the farm while she and her mother and sisters helped to keep the house clean and tidy.

Slaves were not normally allowed to leave the property where they lived, but Martha's father was also a preacher and so he was allowed to go to different places to tell other slaves about God. Sometimes he got paid for his preaching. He saved and saved until he had what he needed to get all of his family out of slavery.

In 1830, when she was about 13 years old, Martha and her family left America and sailed to a new country in West Africa which had been founded as a place for former slaves from America to go and live in freedom. They settled in a township called Clay-Ashland.

Once they arrived there, the family were given some land to farm. Martha and her brothers and sisters could at last go to school, learn how to read and write, and do sums and arithmetic. Martha was very happy to be able to go to school.

The family farmed their land and sold the extra produce and vegetables in the local market in the nearby town. The town was on the coast, and one day while they were there, Martha saw some big sailing ships with rows of cannons.

"What are those ships doing?" she said. She was told that the ships were part of the British Royal Navy.

They patrolled the seas to stop slavers attacking the ships that were bringing the freed slaves to West Africa. If the slavers attacked the ships, they would take everyone on the boat and sell them back into slavery. From then on, Martha was very glad whenever she saw the heavily armed navy boats.

Shortly after they had arrived in Clay-Ashland, a terrible fever broke out and infected everyone living there. Sadly many people died, including Martha's mother, father, and sisters. Her eldest brother had to look after his younger brothers and Martha.

When she was older, Martha met and married a man called Zion Harris. They were farmers and grew crops, as well as raising ducks and sheep.

But one morning the town they lived in was attacked by an African leader called Gotorah. He and his men wanted to kidnap everyone who lived there and sell them back into slavery. Everyone tried to stop the attackers. Eventually Gotorah was shot and killed and his men ran away.

After this attack, Martha and Zion decided to go and live next to a town where they hoped it would be safer. Sadly, Zion died not long after this while he was still quite young.

Some years later, Martha met and married another man, Henry Ricks. They lived happily on a farm where they grew coffee, ginger, and cotton.

Martha still loved to see the navy ships in the port and had found out that Queen Victoria wanted slaves to be free. In 1833, following many years of arguments, the British parliament finally voted to abolish slavery in all of the places it ruled.

Martha decided that she wished to go and see Queen Victoria, to thank her for sending the ships to help and protect them.

Martha was very good at needlework and decided that she would make Queen Victoria a quilt. Her dream was to give it to the Queen as a gift when they met.

No one ever expected that Martha would travel all the way from Africa and actually meet Queen Victoria, but Martha held on to her dream for many, many years.

Martha decorated the quilt with a coffee tree, leaves, and coffee beans, like the ones that grew on her farm. She stitched hundreds of green leaves and red coffee beans on it. She continued making it for over 20 (twenty) years, until finally she had finished it.

Still, no one ever expected Martha's dream to come true. Many years later, however, when she was quite old, Martha was visited by Jane Roberts, the wife of the president of the country. Jane had heard about Martha's dream and the quilt that she had made. Jane decided that she would try to help Martha.

Jane and Martha sailed across the sea to Britain, where Martha's story was published in a British newspaper. It was read by lots of people, including Queen Victoria herself. She was so impressed with Martha's story that she invited Martha to meet her at her palace in Windsor.

So Martha did indeed end up meeting Queen Victoria and giving her the quilt she had made.

Unfortunately, the quilt has been lost, but it was the first quilt to be given as a gift from a West-African country to the queen of another country.

In 2005, Africa's first elected female president, Ellen Johnson Sirleaf, heard about Martha and her gift and decided to continue to give quilts as presents to important visitors.